RESET & RESTART

7 Steps to Enjoy Motherhood Guilt Free,
Fulfil Your Passion and Attain Work Life Balance

RESET & RESTART

7 Steps to Enjoy Motherhood Guilt Free,
Fulfil Your Passion and Attain Work Life Balance

DIVYA GUPTA
TEDx Speaker, Serial Entrepreneur
Co-founder of India's No. 1 Maternity Fashion Brand, MOMZJOY
Director, K R Mangalam School, Delhi/NCR

Worldwide Published by
Pendown Press

PENDOWN PRESS LLP
An ISO 9001 & ISO 14001 Certified Co.,
Regd. Office: 3767A, Kanhaiya Nagar,
Tri Nagar, Delhi-110035
Ph.: 8130886000, 9650072927, 8595249536
E-mail: info@pendownpress.com
Branch Office: 1A/2A, 20, Hari Sadan, Ansari Road,
Daryaganj, New Delhi-110002
Ph.: 011-45794768
Website: PendownPress.com

First Edition: 2024
Price: ₹399/-
ISBN: 978-93-5554-818-4

Layout and Cover Designed by Pendown Graphics Team
Printed and Bound in India by Thomson Press India Ltd.

Dedication

This book is dedicated to my children Avyaan and Avir Gupta, Also to my lifelines Aavya & Aariv Gupta. You all are true blessings in my life, always inspiring me to do my best and live my dreams.

To my husband, Prashant Gupta, for encouraging me to share my experiences and encourage fellow mothers to live their lives to their full potential while enjoying the joy and responsibilities of motherhood. Thank you for being my biggest support and cheerleader!

To my grandparents, OP Gupta (Bauji), Bimla Devi Gupta (Maji), My Nana-Nani, for raising me and my siblings with core ethical values.

To my parents, Rashmi & Braham Dev Gupta; Poonam & Anil Gupta, for being my strongest support system and being the best grandparents to my children.

To my brothers and sisters, Kritika & Akash, Divya C. & Anshul, Deepanshu, Saurabh, Arush, Monica, Ankita, Priyanka, Megha, Shivani, Priya, Karan, Akshay, Siddarth, Prachi, Sarthak, Aastha, Arpit, Pankhuri, Vrinda and Tanish.

To my childhood friend and partner, Kriti Baveja, for embarking on my first entrepreneurial journey with me, and what a fun ride it has been together!

To my friends and family- you know who you are. Thank you for being you !

CONTENTS

FOREWORD

You know that idea of perfectly balancing work and home life? Well, it's kind of a myth. Instead, it's more like a constant juggling act, trying to figure out what's most important at any given moment.

I have known Divya for a couple of years now as a fellow entrepreneur and mom in the same space. I have always been impressed with her speed of implementation.Her ability to manage work and at the same time focus on her health, kids, and work is truly amazing. I have always been keen to know how she manages it all and I'm so glad she has documented it for the benefit of so many mothers out there.

In her book, Divya breaks down how women can tackle this constant juggling act with confidence. She tells us that it's okay not to have everything perfectly balanced all the time. Instead, we should focus on what's important right now.

Drawing from her own experiences as a working mom, Divya gives us practical tips and encourages us to pursue our passions while still taking care of ourselves and our responsibilities at home. She shows us that we can be successful in both our personal and professional lives.

As I read through Divya's book, I felt inspired. Her words reminded me of how we have the power to shape our own lives and find joy in the journey.

I highly recommend this book to any woman who is on the journey of finding her work-life balance. Let Divya's words be your guide as you navigate through this journey.

Malika Sadani
Investor, Founder - The Moms Co.
Mother of 2

ABOUT THE AUTHOR

- Computer engineer from Thapar University, Patiala, India

- MSc Management, Imperial College London Business School

- 2 years of family business work experience withOkaya& Microtek Group

- TEDx Speaker

- Imperial Alumni Entrepreneur Award, 2022

- Listed among Asia's top 50 e-commerce specialists

- Recognized in BusinessWorld's list of 30 under 30

- National Entrepreneur Award Winner

- Investor in the Delhi Government Business Blaster Program

- Maternity Fashion Expert

- Co-launched Momzjoy with childhood friend Kriti Baveja, bootstrapped and profitable, with no prior design or manufacturing experience- today, India's No. 1 Maternity Fashion Brand

- Winner of the Best Maternity Wear Brand Award by Kidstoppress, India's leading parenting portal (5 years in a row: 2016, 2017, 2018, 2019, 2022); Voted by mothers

- Trusted by over 1.3 Lakh moms

- Maintains a strong social media community reaching over a million moms every month

- Empowered mothers in over 43 countries, covering 17000 pin codes in India

- Dressed celebrities such as Sania Mirza, Soha Ali Khan, Swara Bhaskar, Bharti Singh, and many more

TEDx SPEAKER

Babysteps To Success | Divya Gupta | TEDxTIET - YouTube

Divya Gupta, Co-founder Momzjoy, is an avid entrepreneur. Divya pursued her passion to carve out a niche in the Maternity and Nursing ...

HIGHLY COMMENDED, ALUMNI ENTREPRENEUR AWARD, 2021

- **First to launch festive Indian wear, photoshoot gowns, and various disruptive product categories**

National Awardee & Voted by moms as best maternity brand 5 years in a row

INVESTOR, BUSINESS BLASTER, GOVT. OF DELHI INITIATIVE

WHO IS THIS BOOK FOR?

This book is for the following individuals:

- Any individual who is aiming to reach his/her goals.

- Pregnant mothers worrying about how life will change and how they will manage post-delivery.

- New mothers adjusting to new life.

- Mommies experiencing a certain type of void in their lives.

- Women experiencing postpartum depression.

- Couples trying to conceive or wanting to have children, fearing the unknown.

- Ambitious women wanting more from life.

- Homemakers wanting a sense of fulfilment, personal growth, and peace of mind.

- Mom-preneurs struggling to balance it all.

WHY THIS BOOK?

Motherhood is a beautiful journey, but often, it can be extremely lonely and mentally taxing. Your entire world changes and revolves around your little bundle of joy. It is the most precious bond for sure, and I'm sure you would agree with that sentiment.

Agree or not, women are the primary care takers. Most of us get so immersed in taking care of our kids, partners, families, and homes that we forget or compromise with our dreams; and we end up losing ourselves in the process.

Trust me, I speak from experience.

Postpartum depression is real. Struggling to balance kids, home, work, and workouts is real. Reminding yourself of what you really want from life is also a reality.

Hi, my name is **Divya Gupta. I am TEDx Speaker and have worked closely with over 2700 pregnant mothers, new mothers, and doctors.** I am the mother of 2 beautiful children, Avyaan & Avir, who have transformed me as a human. Over the years, I have successfully used certain tools (which I will reveal to you today) to grow myself as an individual post-delivery. After having two babies, I felt more productive and had laser-sharp focus.

I have lost 25kgs post-pregnancy and built my best body, which is strong, nourished, and in shape (and I'm extremely proud of myself for this :D). **I have also grown my business and reported a 4x profit and unmatched customer experience and value while being a full-time working mom! I am a speaker, author, fitness enthusiast, reader, and a full-time mom :)** The journey so far has been brilliant!

You might be wondering why I'm sharing these tools with you today in the form of a book.

Well, in my journey, **I often get asked how I do what I do... How I balance work, home, kids, and workouts.** I have shared my actions with over 55 women in my circle on calls. **Some experienced depression, some were lost, some wanted to start a business but lacked courage, some did not have any support...diverse lives but same question!**

That's when I thought to compile a book of my framework that has worked like magic for me. I am unable to reach everyone personally, **so my gift to moms is this book, which shares valuable lessons that I unearthed over time during my journey of reaching my full potential and experiencing true fulfilment at each stage of my life.**

I hope these sessions will guide you to the path of completeness and success in any area you wish for.

So, without further ado, let's explore 7 fail-proof steps to unlock your full potential while embracing the joy and responsibilities of motherhood.

Mother of Two, Serial Entrepreneur,
Fitness Enthusiast

Divya Gupta

MINDSET SHIFT

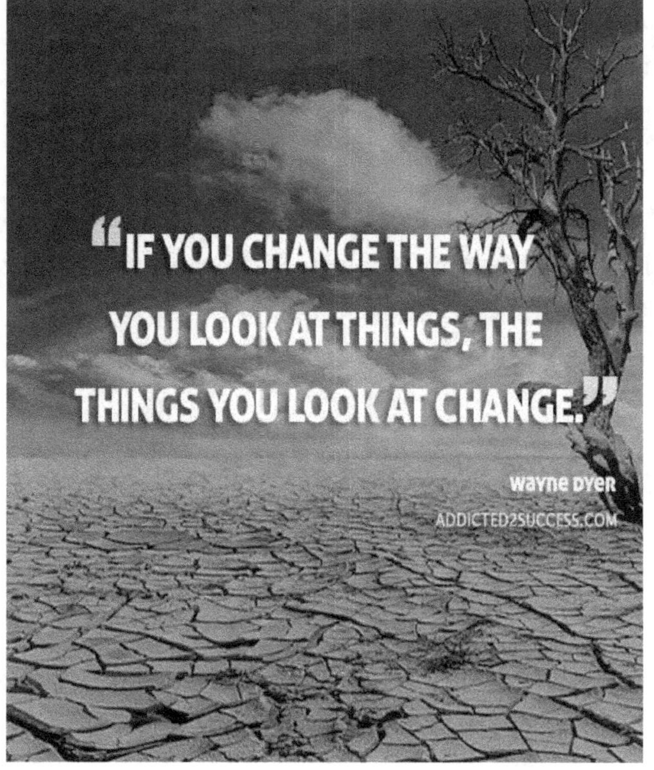

1.1 IS IT POSSIBLE?

It is commonly believed that women have to choose between their dreams and being a good mother. If you are ambitious or outgoing, you are labelled as a bad mom. If you want to pursue a passion, you are labelled as selfish. If you are a home maker and take out some time for yourself, you are labelled as careless.

Achieving your Dreams Vs being a Great Mom??

But the truth is, you can have both. Yes, you read it right-It is possible to be the best mother (in fact, you are the best mother anyway!) and fulfil your dreams. And guess what? All mothers are the best mothers. There is absolutely no bad mom concept- it is just a label!

And this joy of not losing yourself while being a great mother is priceless. You have to BELIEVE- that it is possible. And if you can see it, you can do it!

1.2 KNOW WHAT YOU TRULY WANT

More than 80% of people live their lives without knowing what they really want from life. We are often too busy to take the time to write down our goals and plan our lives. And this gives us a feeling of emptiness, with a constant sense that something is missing.

The major difference between star achievers and the rest of us is that WE DONT KNOW WHAT WE WANT... WE DONT KNOW WHAT MAKES US HAPPY, TRULY HAPPY!

So, take out one day, and write all your goals, wishes, desires in a diary or digital media. Pen down your thoughts and you will fell so much lighter. You don't need to start working on all your goals at once; prioritize them and set some aside for later. But start with listing them.

1.3 ZERO EXPECTATIONS

I have observed that we waste 90% of our time in personal grudges. We have certain expectations from all people around us, and when these are not met, we feel let down. This feeling occupies so much mental space that it actually has a gradual effect on our health and other relationships too.

No relationship is perfect, but I strongly believe that all humans are good souls at the core. It is difficult, but if you can rise above trivial matters and continue to give your best to the relationships that matter without expecting anything in return, you will actually build a stronger bond and experience greater peace of mind.

Stay away from those who give you negative vibes or drain your energy, but love your selected ones fully with ZERO EXPECTATIONS!

1.4 100% I, 0% YOU

Achievers don't play the blame game. They don't give reasons for things not done. It all starts with YOU and only you. When you take charge and believe that your life is in your control, your mindset changes drastically, and you become a go-getter. You are exactly where you should be because of your choices. For example,

- I want to get fit, **BUT** I have no time.

- I love to paint, **BUT** I have not painted since the last 5 years.

- Now, just replace this **'BUT'** with **'AND'** and see the MAGIC.

- I want to get fit, **AND** I have no time.

- I love to paint, **AND** I have not painted since the last 5 years.

In the first case, we can see mind blocks, but when we replace our thoughts with AND, we get two situations, and we can now find a solution. Say, for example, I want to get fit, and I have no time, so let me see why I have no time. Can I wake up a bit earlier, or can I delegate a task to someone else so I can work out in that time, or can I start with a 15-minute walk to begin with? The moment there is a mindset shift, the entire game changes.

SELF CARE

> "An empty lantern provides no light. Self-care is the fuel that allows your light to shine brightly."
>
> — UNKNOWN

2.1 NOURISH YOUR BODY

Our body is truly magical. It can create a tiny human, something that no one else can do. And in that process, our body changes drastically. We should not expect our bodies to return to its pre-pregnancy size soon after giving birth. Some women are surprised that their stomach looks 4-5 months pregnant even after delivery. But try not to worry, as this is because the uterus (the womb), which expanded throughout the nine months of pregnancy to make space for the growing baby, needs time (typically 6-8 weeks) to return to its normal size. Extra fluid built up inside the pregnant body also decreases gradually, thereby reducing swelling and bloating.

It is natural to have negative feelings about our post-baby body. Trust me- I feel you. I had a real hard time looking at myself in the mirror post-pregnancy. We feel the pressure and desire to look a certain way, but the reality is that most bodies change post-baby birth and need time to recover and gain strength. So try not to compare yourself with anyone as all bodies are different. All journeys are different too.

It is essential to **nourish your body with the right food, vitamins, minerals, and calcium post-delivery.** This gives you strength to get back to normal life. Whether it's a C-section or normal delivery, in both cases, a woman must pay utmost priority to her health by **visiting the doctor for supplements, planning a diet that covers all nutrients, and** seeking **breastfeeding support totruly nourish the body.**

No one can help you like yourself, so don't wait for anyone to do this for you. Take charge to heal yourself in all ways and be your best version! Just see how much you will enjoy each precious moment with your child then.

- **Sunlight & fresh air-** for your daily Vitamin-D requirements and mood upliftment. Just go for a stroll and see the magic of this "me-time"!

- **Food supplements -** to address all deficiencies in the body post-pregnancy.

- **Nutritious food -** helps to regain strength and promotes breastfeeding.

- **Body massage -** it relaxes all muscles and relieves pain.

2.2 WATER INTAKE

We all agree that a healthy diet is very important for a healthy pregnancy. However, hydration is often overlooked. Water transports nutrients, regulates body temperature, eliminates waste, and improves digestion. All these functions are key in developing a healthy baby.

Here are some ways to help you make it easier to stay hydrated.

- Add fruits like raspberries/watermelon slices to your water.

- Avoid caffeine.

- Increase fruit and vegetable intake (as well as other foods with high water content).

- Milk, juice, tea, sparkling water, and soup all are additional sources of water.

- Listen to your body; when you feel thirsty, make sure you drink water.

- Drink enough fluids to make your urine colorless or light yellow.

- Avoid intense heat.

- Increase fluid intake before and during an increase in activity.

- Drink water after waking up.

2.3 POWER OF DEEP SLEEP

Sleep becomes a distant dream after having a baby!

While 7-8 hours of sleep is highly recommended for all individuals, the challenge is that a new mother's schedule is dependent on that of the child. Some babies sleep in parts, some sleep through the day and are active at night, and some wake up as soon as the mommy sleeps :p

What worked for me was a simple advice from my mother- Sleep when your baby sleeps and let other members of the house take care of the household chores. If you have a support system, then this really works like magic. I started by getting 6-7 hours of sleepin parts and mentally would think that 7 hours of sleep is complete, so its fine...It really pushed me to have a productive day instead of just thinking all day that I hadn't slept.

Slowly, the sleep cycle starts getting better, especially after 3 months post-delivery. After a year, it gets almost normal, with few exceptions when the child is active at night. But try to get your power naps and deep sleep at night. Your partner and family can be a huge support here. Nothing heals better than sleep, so make it a priority.

2.4 EXERCISE AS A LIFESTYLE CHANGE

After both my pregnancies, I gained 25 kgs plus. In the last two weeks, I stopped checking my weight as standing on the weighing scale would shock me every time. After my delivery, I lost 3 kgs only. I had no strength to hold the baby. My back would hurt, my wrists were in immense pain, and my stamina was zero.

I waited for 3 months post-delivery to start working out. until then, I rested well and nourished my body with good food and ladoos, everything that our grandma suggests we should have. At 3 months, I started my workout journey, aiming not only for weight loss but also for strength and a good mood. Mamas, the journey was too hard and challenging. After 2-3 squats, I would give up.

I started going for walks and was determined to dedicate one hour to exercising with my super talented postnatal trainer. Her confidence in me, and my consistency, helped me lose the extra kilos within 6 months of working out. Before my baby was one year old, I was back to my pre-pregnancy weight, and more importantly, I could lift my baby easily and had the stamina to play and be my best around him.

In this journey, I just fell in love with fitness. It has now become a part of my lifestyle. I naturally choose healthy eating options, stay active throughout the day and try to work out 5-6 days a week, otherwise, I feel so incomplete. Exercise is like meditation for me now. It is my time with myself where I feel every muscle, every body part, and thank it for creating magic everyday.

Trust me, we all have reasons not to work out, but find your 'one reason' to exercise daily; one hour is just 4% of your day, so no excuses. It really is not an option for anyone. The benefits are immense, and it has to be a part of our lifestyle now. Find your support group or workout buddies and just enjoy the journey. Results will follow :)

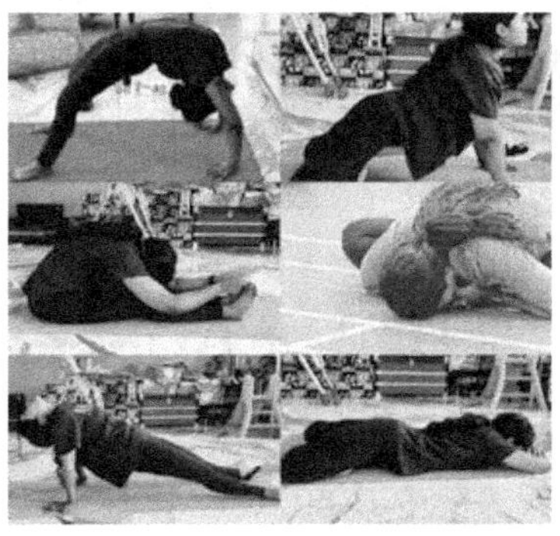

2.5 PAMPER YOURSELF

A Happy mama is the most beautiful! And when we're happy, we raise happy kids too. Happiness is the ultimate aim of life, right? At whatever stage we are in life, we must pamper ourselves, because why not?

Some suggestions to pamper yourself are here:

- Go for a good spa with your girlfriends.

- Brunching with your girls and catching up is a great way to unwind.

- Spend a few days with your partner or friends, with or without kids; it can be a great break from your routine.

- Enjoy a cup of hot coffee and a nice book at a cafe!

- Simply chilling in a garden outdoors- what a feeling in the sun and fresh air!

- Watch Netflix or enjoy a stand- up comedy session for a good laugh riot.

2.6 MEDITATION

Meditation is the most powerful habit we can build and teach the next generation too. It is such a good tool to fight all problems in life and to stay focused and realize our full potential. You can start with 10 minutes of meditation and gradually extend the time as you enjoy the benefits and the experience.

Meditation during pregnancy has multiple benefits for both the mother and the baby. It emits positive vibes and makes us more self-aware. A new mom may feel exhausted and depressed during her journey. This stress, combined with guilt, leads to anxiety. However, we can reduce the negative feelings and increase patience with this super powerful tool - MEDITATION. It will help us manage emotions better.

The emotional and physical benefits of meditation can include:

- Giving you a new way to look at things that cause stress
- Building skills to manage your stress
- Making you more self-aware
- Focusing on the present
- Reducing negative feelings
- Enhancing creativity
- Helping you be more patient

2.7 DRESS WELL

Did you know that it's actually possible to feel very confident and energetic and attract the right kind of people if one is dressed well?

I understand and relate to the thought we have most of the time when we feel that confidence is about the mind more than any external factor. However, over the past few years of working with women, being an entrepreneur, and creative myself, I've come to learn that there are a great many benefits to making the effort to dress well.

Dressing well has been shown to have a positive impact on our health, both mentally and physically. One way that dressing well can improve health is by boosting our confidence. When we feel good and stylish, we may feel more self-assured and capable of tackling challenges. In contrast, if we stay in clumsy pyjamas and are not groomed, we may feel unwell and non-productive.

Someone told me once- **"Why do we keep waiting to get to our best shape to dress well?"** Dressing up makes us feel good about ourselves regardless of our shape and size. Embrace it and enjoy it because you are worth it!

CHILD CARE

"CHILDREN ARE NOT
A DISTRACTION FROM MORE
IMPORTANT WORK.
THEY ARE THE
MOST IMPORTANT WORK."

John Trainer, M.D.
Our Muddy Bootser

3.1 POWER OF ROUTINE

"You'll never change your life until you change something you do daily. The secret of your success is found in your daily routine" — John C. Maxwell

A routine is a series of behaviour that are repeated frequently. Eventually, some routines can become habits.

Small wins everyday result in big wins. Our brain craves for routines and habits. Our dual actions are often driven by unconscious habits that we have developed overtime.

Having a routine is all about discipline. Discipline is one quality that can take us from where we are to where we want to be. Remembering your purpose, creating a path, and then following it in your daily routine is a powerful way to not only achieve your dreams but also to build strong character!

I strongly recommend reading the book "Atomic Habits" by James Clear to create daily habits as a lifestyle change.

Having a routine is not very complicated. I'm sharing my simple routine here which I try follow but sometimes miss:

- 5:00 am- Wake up

- 5:30 to 6:30 am- Workout online with a trainer (Having a mentor keeps me consistent)

- 6:30-7:30 am- Get kids ready for school

- 7:30 am- Leave for work

- 2:00 pm- Reach home and have lunch with kids

- 3:00-4:00 pm- Free time

- 4:00-5:00 pm- Fun activity with kids or read books or practice writing

- 5:00-6:00 pm- Class or play time

- 6:00-7:00 pm- Dinner and family time

- 8:00-9:00 pm- Put kids to sleep

- 9:00-10:00 pm- Read a book and go to sleep

Once a mother, always a mother- and our routine is mostly created around our core responsibilities such as managing the children, taking care of the house, our workplace and relationships. Also, there will be many situations where we might not be able to follow our routine, but we must keep trying to resume it and make it a habit.

3.2 DEVELOP A SUPPORT SYSTEM

It takes an entire village to raise a kid! This saying that we have all heard just makes so much sense once you become a parent.

Stop taking all the pressure yourself and trying to find a solution alone every time. This was my major struggle, and sometimes still is; I don't ask for help!

I am slowly learning that it is okay to talk your heart out and ask for help. Support is all around us; we need to reach out.

I conveyed how I felt and how I was struggling to manage time with my partner. Surpassingly, the situation became much lighter when we decided to make changes to our schedule so that both of us could balance work and home.

I reached out to my parents, and they were more than happy to help me. Sometimes we just assume and sometimes there is no support- but there is always a way! Look for a solution inside or outside family. Adjust your timings according to child's schedule, and it really helps.

According to research, a strong support system has many positive benefits. Some of the best benefits include higher levels of well-being, better coping skills, and a longer, healthier life. It reduces depression, anxiety, and stress.

So, develop your support system and take charge of your life, girl!

If you have any situation where you can't find your support system, feel free to write to me at divya@momzjoy.com, and I assure you I will work with you to solve it!

3.3 USE CHECKLISTS

A checklist is a list of things you must do or have. This simple list is so powerful that a well-designed checklist can save your hours of hard work and stress. It reduces the tendency to avoid, omit, and neglect important steps in any task. I use checklists in both my personal and professional life. It's a way of multiplying your productivity.

For example, I have a checklist for the food to be given to my kids daily so that nutrition is covered, including items like:

1# Dry fruits

2# 2 fruits

3# Curd

4# Coconut water

5# Carrot and beetroot salad

6# Makhanas or sprouts

7# Milk with homemade dry fruit powder

My only target is to not miss these throughout the day. I also have a checklist for everything I do; it keeps me clear in my head and helps me declutter:

- My nutrition

- Tasks to check at the office when I work remotely

- Things to buy monthly like restocking grocery and toiletries

- Places to explore with the family in a month

When you list things, you do more with the same time, and one day of planning gives so much value to the entire month.

PRODUCTIVITY

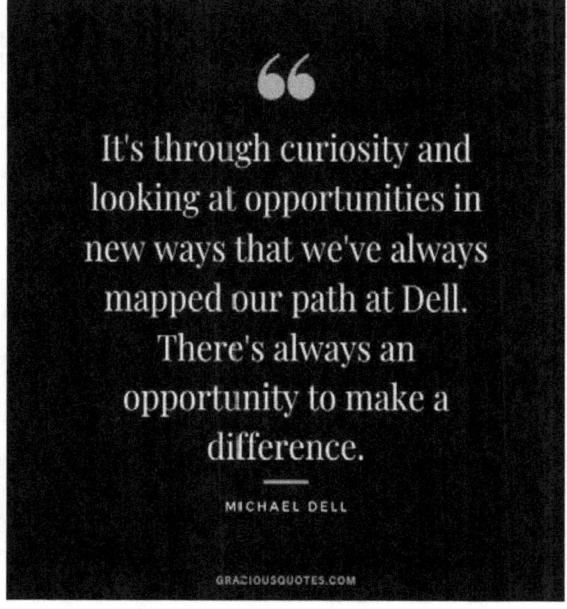

We all have the same amount of time. What makes some people more successful is knowing how to make better use of it or

4.1 QUALITY OVER QUANTITY

Children want our undivided attention, our time. We mean the world to them until 10 years of age at least. We might have a big circle, priorities and a big world, but to them, it's just us!

When it comes to kids, it's not the quantity but the quality of time that matters. All they want is our undivided attention, even if it's just for one hour everyday. As they grow up, they won't remember what toy or game we gifted, but they will remember the time we spent with them.

High-quality time with parents and caregivers- is the most beneficial to children and can have a positive effect on them as they grow. It isn't about endless hours of time—it's about how you choose to spend that time that truly matters.

Spending 15 minutes reading a book with your baby snuggled in your lap, asking questions, and acting out the characters is better than being in the same room with your baby for an hour while your baby plays and you smile at her every so often.

So, if you worry that you're not spending enough time with your child, remember to make the moments you do have together count by being present and engaged with your little one.

The same principle is applicable to work as well. Give quality time to whatever you give your attention to, and you will see the magic!

4.2 NO TIME IS NO EXCUSE

We all have 24 hours in a day! How we use it makes all the difference.

Will you allow me to share a harsh truth? Not everyone will accept this, but those who do will never be the same again.

"I don't have time" is just an excuse your brain creates to keep you stuck in your comfort zone. Connect to your why is the key to get past it. Remember your purpose. When you make something a priority, you will find the time for it.

The reverse is also true- When something is not your priority, it never gets done.

Do you know?

Work not done + Reasons = (is not) Work done

Replace your 'BUT' with 'AND' as we discussed before, and you will find a way, or you will continue to live a wishful life with regrets.

So, I urge you - I sincerely urge you - to make this mindset shift. Make yourself so headstrong that if you want something, you will find a way to get it :)

4.3 THE ART OF SCHEDULING

Wow, this is my favourite topic. I love scheduling. Infact, I thrive on it. I receive so many messages on Instagram and LinkedIn asking me how I balance work, home, kids, and workouts... I always tell them: the only thing that makes it possible for me to dare to dream while giving full time to my growing children as well is scheduling.

Scheduling is the art of planning your activities so that you can achieve your goals and priorities in the time you have available. When it's done effectively, it helps you understand what you can realistically achieve with your time.

There are many apps that help in scheduling- I love Google Calendar and sync it with all my gadgets. You can try any app that you are comfortable with. But when you put everything in your calendar, it gets done. If not in the calendar, it will happen when you recall, which is a matter of chance.

If you want to create a productive daily schedule that meets your specific needs, follow these steps:

1# Write everything down.

2# Identify priorities.

3# Note the frequency.

4# Cluster similar tasks.

5# Make a weekly chart.

6# Optimize your tasks.

7# Order the tasks.

8# Stay flexible- put enough gaps also to avoid overlap.

4.4 BATCHING

Batching is another powerful tool to boost your productivity by 10x.

But what actually is BATCHING?

It is the act of grouping tasks together, so you do them all at once, instead of switching tasks that take place at different times, thereby consuming more time.

How do I use it?

I list all things I do in a day, and then I group them together.

For Example: I make all my phone calls while going to pick up my kids from school or while walking to complete my daily step target.

I plan the menu for the week every Sunday so that I don't have to think about it daily, and I can plan better nutrition by adding all food groups to the week.

Batching saves immense time and energy, making you much more productive. Getting more done in less time, which is much needed after motherhood, is possible with this simple trick.

So, make your lists now, group them together, and assign a day to them - like doing all buying and scheduling on weekends, and certain tasks throughout the day at fixed times.

If this benefits you, don't forget to share with us so that it inspires more of us and encourages others to use it too!

4.5 LONG LISTS DONT WORK

Long to-do lists don't work.FACT CHECK!

Make smaller to-do lists and get things done. Small wins account for big results. When was the last time you completed a long to-do list? We tend to complete initial tasks, and then the list gets lost, leaving us with an incomplete feeling. But when you complete small lists, mentally you feel like you have accomplished something and had a productive day. Long lists are guilt trips! When you feel bad about them, eventually you stop looking at the lists, and the whole thing stresses you out.

The better way is to break it into small task lists. When you complete it, at least 1% of your long list is complete. This smaller picture makes you feel motivated and gives you satisfaction. You can then move on to the other 1% of the long list.

In general, whenever you feel stuck, write down everything and divide the problem into smaller pieces until you can deal with them quickly. Rearranging the task list itself has a major impact on our productivity and motivation.

ALL ABOUT MOM GUILT

My home being a mess

Taking time for myself

Feeding my child(ren) the same thing daily

My big reactions or raising my voice

Using technology more than I "should"

Pursuing my career

Not being able to give my child more opportunities because of finances

Not giving my child my undivided attention

5.1 IT IS BETWEEN YOU AND YOUR CHILD

Mom guilt is real... I have gone through it. In fact, I feel every mom goes through mom guilt at some point in time.

When we are with children, many times we feel like we are missing out on life! And vice versa happens as well. When we are at work or traveling, we deeply miss our children and mom guilt creeps in.

But you know what?

Surround yourself with supportive people and shake off the rest.

There is nothing wrong with avoiding people or relatives who make you feel judged or guilty.

There is no permanent solution to it, but following can help:

- Remember, it is between you and your child. Don't let what others say get to your mind.

- Identify what you feel guilty about and put it into words.

- Acknowledge that there are no rules or requirements.

- Make a choice! You have to choose to be happy and drop the guilt factors.

All mothers are best for their children. All parents do their best, so let's acknowledge it. And let's also stop judging other moms and friends ourselves.

5.2 SOCIAL MEDIA IS TOXIC

Well, this is my favourite topic!

Social media has many benefits, but spending too much time on it and consuming certain types of content can make a lot of difference. Social media apps and games are addictive and consume our time and mental energy.

Spending hours watching never-ending reels or content can lead us to compare ourselves to everyone we see online, which can be damaging to our mental health.

Did you know that social media can also affect our physical health?

Researchers have found a connection between the mind and the gut, which can turn anxiety and depression into headaches, muscle tension, and other physical symptoms.

Here are some simple practical tips to reduce social media use:

- Limit your use to once or twice a day.

- If you can control the urge, consider deleting the app (not your account). Having to reinstall the app each time you want to use it will make you think twice and reduce the urge to constantly check.

- Of course, the best option is to delete your account altogether, but if you're not ready for that step, you can still filter the content you see and restrict your time on social media.

Just keep these pointers in mind, and you can embark on a practical DIGITAL DETOX!

5.3 OVER SOCIALISING IS TOXIC

Having a supportive network of family and friends helps us relieve stress. However, it is also important to acknowledge the fact that too much socialising can sometimes be overwhelming and lead to anxiety and stress. We tend to feel that the grass is greener on the other side and everyone has a perfect life. This gives rise to major FOMO (fear of missing out), and we start feeling depressed about our own lives.

Too much socialising can also lead to losing focuson our goals and purpose, causing us to get carried away. Therefore, maintaining the right balance is critical. Go out, meet people, avoid comparisons and stay focused. This way, you can socialise mindfully.

REST. RESET. RESTART

Rest.
Reset.
Restart.
Refocus.
As many times
as you need to.

———

6.1 REST. RESET. RESTART. REPEAT

I don't know how many times I have done this, but it works like magic everytime. Whenever I feel overwhelmed or confused and need clarity, I take a break, write everything on paper, and then analyze my thoughts. After that, I am ready to restart.

In life, when something is not working, we have to reset it...

It's absolutely okay to reset, refocus, reschedule, and re-do things to make them better, feel better, and live better. If you feel off-balance, go somewhere where you can find peace and then get back at it. Hit the reset button, restart, or refocus as many times as you need to in order to figure out your calling, identity, and purpose in life.

Life is a journey with ups and downs, and we have to adjust to different phases of life. Start fresh, start again, and take a few days to rest to get your minds right. Get your mind right, and then get your life on track. It all starts with you, so take control of your yourself - Your life, Your choices. If something is not working, start again and again and again.

It's much better than giving up, and it will make you happier!

6.2 Reflect and Learn

After taking a break and resetting, it's crucial to reflect on the experiences and lessons learned. Reflecting allows us to gain insights into what worked well, what didn't, and how we can improve moving forward. Learning from our experiences helps us grow and adapt more effectively in the future.

6.3 Seek Support and Guidance

During times of reset and restart, reaching out for support and guidance can be incredibly beneficial. Whether it's seeking advice from a mentor, confiding in a trusted friend, or seeking professional help, having a support system can provide valuable perspective and encouragement along the way.

REMEMBER YOUR WHY

7.1 Reconnecting with Your Goals and Aspirations

In the hustle and bustle of daily life, it's easy to lose sight of our long-term goals and aspirations. Take a moment to pause and reflect on what truly matters to you. What are your dreams for yourself and your family? Whether it's achieving career milestones, providing a better life for your children, or making a positive impact in your community, your goals serve as a beacon of light, guiding you towards a brighter future.

As you think about your goals and dreams, ask yourself why they matter to you. Imagine how achieving them could make your life, your family's life, and even the world better. Visualize the person you want to become as you work towards your dreams, and think about the values and passions that drive you forward. By doing this, you can stay focused and motivated. Every small step you take toward your goals gets you closer to making your dreams come true. So, stay focused, stay positive, and keep moving forward with confidence in your ability to create the life you desire.

7.2 Finding Strength and Motivation

Your "why" is deeply personal and unique to you. It's the driving force behind every decision you make and every action you take. By staying connected to your "why," you can find the strength and motivation to overcome any obstacle that comes your way. Remember the dreams you're chasing, the values you're upholding, and the legacy you're building. Let your "why" be your guiding light, leading you towards a life of purpose and fulfillment.

In moments of doubt or difficulty, it's natural to question our path and wonder if we have what it takes to keep going. That's when reconnecting with your "why" becomes even more crucial. Take time to revisit the moments of joy, passion, and fulfillment that inspired your goals in the first place. Reflect on the impact you hope to make, not just on yourself but also on the lives of those around you.

Believe in the importance of what you're doing to help you move forward, knowing that each little step you take brings you nearer to the life you want for yourself.

7.3 Embracing the Journey

Being a working mom is an exciting journey, full of surprises and challenges. It's like going on a thrilling ride where you experience highs and lows, but you're never alone because your family is right there with you. Sometimes, you might feel really tired or overwhelmed, but it's important to remember why you're doing it all.

Even when things get tough, think about what motivates you – whether it's providing for your family or chasing your dreams. And always stay true to yourself and what you believe in. Nobody's perfect, so don't worry about trying to be. Just embrace your journey, learn from the experiences, and enjoy every precious moment along the way. You'll find strength and joy in the journey, both at work and at home.

SUMMARY

Firstly, congratulations for reaching this far! You did it!

If you are reading this, it means that you have the determination to make your own life, live without reasons, and make it happen, no matter how challenging it may look right now. I assure you- your dreams will come true, and you will achieve what you desire!

Next, let's have deep gratitude for this life. We are exactly where we should be. It is a blessing, mama.

Thank you to our body, our family, our children, and our support system for keeping it all together.

Now you just have to keep it simple:

1# 1. MIND SHIFT Believe what you want is possible. If you can dream it, you can do it!

2# 2. SELF-CARE

    a. Food

    b. Water intake

    c. Supplements

   d. Movement

   e. Meditation

3# CHILD CARE

4# Productivity

   a. Batching

   b. Checklist

   c. Scheduling

5# MOM Guilt

6# REST. RESET. RESTART. REPEAT

   a. 6.1 REST. RESET. RESTART. REPEAT

   b. 6.2 Reflect and Learn

   c. 6.3 Seek Support and Guidance

7# Remember Your Why

   a. ● Reconnecting with Your Goals and Aspirations

   b. ● Finding Strength and Motivation

   c. ● Embracing the Journey

Trust me, I speak from experience.

Sharinghere few inspirational stories of moms who achieved their dreams after embracing motherhood. I Hope they inspire you as much as they inspired me.

TWO PATHS

Dear mommies, we now have two options:

First option is to stay as is and just go with the flow. Go where life takes you and look back 15-20 years down the line, hoping that things would have been different.

Or

Second option is to carve your own way. Take life where you want to go. Make no excuse. Give no reason. MAKE IT HAPPEN! No one will come to change your life on your behalf. GET UP AND GET MOVING! Take charge.

RESET & RESTART

BOTH OPTIONS ARE HARD. CHOOSE YOUR HARD

CONCLUSION

We discussed the 7 steps in detail to unlock our full potential. The fundamentals remain the same; the interpretation and implementation may vary according to your individual needs over the years. For example, today you might be struggling to find time for yourself with a newborn baby. Tomorrow, you might find it challenging to balance your teenage kid's needs and your passion. The situation will keep changing, but the core is always the same.

Remember, my friends, this is a journey. It has its ups and downs. But don't forget to **REST, RESET & RESTART** as many times as needed. Our goal is to get better than yesterday, and mark my words: **small wins will amount to big leaps.**

All the best as you embark on your journey of enjoying motherhood to the fullest and also living an awesome life fulfilling all your dreams and passion.

You know I am just a click away for any **personal custom support** that you might require (email: divya@momzjoy.com). I would love to discuss with you one-on-one, and I promise that together we will achieve motherhood AND personal growth!

Subscribe to our YouTube channel

(https://www.youtube.com/@momzjoy123)

Visit our website to read like minded valuable blogs

(www.momzjoy.com)

TESTIMONIALS

Mrs Aparna Jain,

Directors, Business Coaching India

Mothers can lead fulfilling lives without sacrificing their dreams. his book explains it in depth with real-life examples in such simple words.

TESTIMONIALS

Ankur Hora

Father and Real Estate Marketing expert

A must-read for all moms who lose themselves after having a baby. Crisp practical tips and tricks revealed so transparently!

TESTIMONIALS

Dr. Mahima Bakshi
Maternal Child Wellness Coach,
Author
Women's Activist, TEDx Speaker, Founder - Birthing
Naturally

Postpartum depression, anxiety, and stress are significant challenges for new mothers. Covering topics like mindset shifts, mom guilt, and providing self-care and child care hacks will undoubtedly have a positive impact on new mothers, potentially reducing their anxiety and postpartum depression.

TESTIMONIALS

Dr. Juhee Jain

MBBS, MD - Obstetrics & Gynaecology

Gynecologist, Obstetrician, Infertility Specialist,

Laparoscopic Surgeon (Obs & Gyn)

Divya talked about a really important topic here. I see many patients who are anxious about life after having children and how they will manage their careers. This worry can even lead to feeling really sad. I'm happy Divya made a plan to help moms in a simple and good way.

TESTIMONIALS

Sanjana Guglani
South Indian Actor
Mother, Entrepreneur, Philanthropist

Loved the powerful productivity hacks shared in the book, especially the concept of batching and the power of routine. I found this book to be much more than just facts!

TESTIMONIALS

Anil Gupta

CEO & Director, Okaya Microtek Group

Divya is leading by example in how to excel in all roles beautifully, which looked effortless to me before reading this book. Now I know how much planning and multitasking women can do.